Top Ten Scopes
To Follow in 2016

Ryan Roy

Table of Contents

Preface

This book is a compilation of ten people I have identified on Periscope to be authentic and consistent. I wish I had a book like this when I first started on Periscope. When I downloaded the Periscope APP, I hit the globe to find content. I clicked on a random Red Dot and came across a Broadcast with a young teenage girl yelling at her 20 viewers for not talking to her and asking questions. My immediate thought was, " Aren't you supposed to be talking to us?" I quickly got off the APP thinking, "I do not think this platform is for me."

It took me over 2 months of researching and watching other scopers, doing over 150 of my own broadcasts and doing both of these things daily (consistently) to find these 10 gems.

I know this is my opinion, but do yourself a favor and follow each of these individuals in this book for a week to see if the resonate with you. If they all do, AMAZING!! If only one does, AMAZING!! That means you did not have to search for 2 months to find that person.

The other reason I wrote this book is self serving. I set a goal to write a book in the first month of the year. Today is January 13, 2016. I reached out to most of the members of this book on January 7, 2016.

That is right; I completed an entire book in less than a week. I have never written or published a book. But when you have the right tools and support anything is possible.

The main resource I purchased was Instant Author.

If you have a story, have thought of writing a book, have a book written and do not know the next step. Well I would highly suggest Instant Author.

My biggest fear was not writing the book. It was the process of publishing the book. Instant Author provided all of the answers in a clear in concise manner. If I could do it, ANYONE can do it.

Go to http://ryanroy.me/book to find more about how to publish your own book too!

Ryan Roy

@JustifyorJustDoIt

 343,571

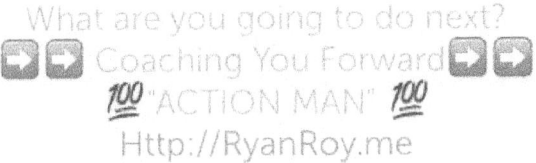

What are you going to do next?
Coaching You Forward
💯 "ACTION MAN" 💯
Http://RyanRoy.me

3	723	310
RECENT	FOLLOWERS	FOLLOWING

Ryan Roy

1. How were you introduced to Periscope?

I was on a coaching call with a first time client. She asked me if I had heard about it. She said I would be great at it. So I looked into it and didn't immediately see the connection. However I didn't ignore the advice either.

2. What was your first Aha Moment when you KNEW you had to scope consistently?

After those first few weeks of knowing about it, I attended a local Meet Up group about Periscope. I saw the POWER of Periscope during that 2-hour meeting. After two weeks of watching broadcasts I bought Michael Cinquinos' course "Livestream Profit Machine." Michael said in the course to scope three times a day for seven days straight. I haven't looked back.

3. What are your scopes about?
I scope about everything. I mainly focus on mindset towards achieving your goals and dreams. When I coach, I often coach about life balance and focusing energy in each area of your life. Health, Relationships, Business and Finances, if you were to hit the FOLLOW button, I believe you would see that my energy also is

balanced in those areas.

4. What can new FOLLOWERS expect from your scopes.

You can expect to see me passionate about people achieving their dreams. There really isn't any fluff. I have good days and bad days, just like you. But I will continue to show up and deliver. Know that I will always appreciate every viewer on my Scopes. Without each and every one of you, my messages have no voice.

5. What do you want your viewers to know about you?

I'm a passionate father and husband first. Then I'm passionate about helping people realize they are amazing and perfect just the way they are. Once they realize how amazing they are, the sky is the limit for them.

6. Why should they click the FOLLOW button?

Reality TV is NOT real. People are tired of being lied to. If you are ready for the Truth, Unedited and Unscripted, HIT THE FOLLOW BUTTON.

How has Periscope helped me? I have made more contacts and amazing people taking massive action in 2 months than I have in the last 4 years. This community breeds success if you chose it to. It can be anything you want it to be. I want it to be a way for me to connect to a larger audience of people who want more success in their lives.

Top Ten Scopes To Follow

Jim Beach

@mrrelentless

❤ 1,219,263

International Motivational Speaker
& Author. Motivating & Inspiration
Daily! PeriNewbies Mentor BAM!
💥 💣 💥 #PeriNewbies http://
Facebook.com/MrRelentless10X

1	2,653	667
RECENT	FOLLOWERS	FOLLOWING

 Following

Jim Beach

1. How were you introduced to Periscope?

I was on Facebook one day and seen an update from one of my friends, Matt Maddix, and it said, "Join me on Periscope LIVE as I share some motivational tips on how to have more energy. I didn't know what Periscope was but I downloaded the app so as to not miss out because he always shares great content. I fell in love with the app and considered using it myself and was hooked.

2. What was your first Aha moment when you KNEW you had to Scope consistently?

When I started scoping I wasn't too sure how it all worked. Learning what the hearts meant was my first step in discovering how to give appreciation for the content and how I had to give great content to receive the same. After a few scopes I noticed my heart count climbing and I realized that I had new followers. I really wanted to get my message out to more so I asked myself, "What do I need to do to get even more followers and share my message with new people?" That's when I started checking out the top scopers I followed and studying what they were doing. Most of them scoped once a day, sometimes twice, and that's when it hit me...I can't share my message and just hope people watch my replay and share the scope, I need to be more consistent and the audience will grow.

3. What are your scopes about?

I scope motivational and inspirational tips on how to go after your goals and dreams with a relentless attitude and how to realize them before they give up. Stories I share come from my own personal life experiences and how I overcame the many challenges I faced so as to inspire others to know that they can overcome their own challenges.

4. What can new FOLLOWERS expect from your scopes?

Those that jump on my scopes, whether live or on the replay, can expect to find motivation and inspiration for their personal growth. I engage so that I can answer questions and encourage on an individual basis. This also makes for fun and interactive scopes.

5. What do you want your viewers to know about you?

I am an International Motivational Speaker, Business Owner, Author, Husband & Dad. My motivational speaking career happened as a result of having noticeable success in the marketing world and was requested to share my story as to how I was doing so well. I am intentional and passionate about helping people achieve their goals and dreams, those things in which they desire and deserve.

6. Why should they click the FOLLOW button?

Giving away free coaching content is often shared on my scopes from which most anyonecan benefit.

Ryan's note:

When I first joined Periscope and I was watching 20 different scopers per day I kept seeing Jim in every room. His name is Mr. Relentless. I said to myself, "This man is not only following everyone, but he is supporting him or her. " I decided to find him on Facebook and ask him to support me. He did just that.   More amazing is Jim has been able to leverage Periscope and gain contact with his mentor Les Brown. Les reached out to Jim when he heard his story through the platform. And is now personally mentoring him. The Power of Periscope is at work for Jim.   I am happy to have witnessed this first hand.

Ask Mama Louise Intuitive Master Life Coach

@alwaysworthy2

 601,729

💞 How to lose your fear & rock your scopes 🔮 Tips on Expanding The Miracles of You 🔮 Leadership Speaker 🔮 Perinewbies 🔮 Peri10k 🔮 Email : askmamalouise@gmail.com

6	1,718	854
RECENT	FOLLOWERS	FOLLOWING

✓ Following

Mama Louise

1. How were you introduced to Periscope?

I was introduced to Periscope by following Ms. Amber Aziza (who is an extraordinary Business Building Coach) on her Face Book group page Midnight Millionaires. I constantly saw her talking about this thing called Periscope so I went on an adventure to find out why she insisted that Periscope was a business gold mine. OMG she was right this magical place called Periscope turned out to be a free education on human compassion in relationships, business building with what you have now and enhancing your personal development in this thing that we call "Life."

2. What was your first Aha moment when you KNEW you had to Scope consistently?

I was watching all of the great speakers from one of the Periscope groups entitled Peri 10k during a star studded Share a thon scope and they all strongly encouraged everyone to move pass their fears and broadcast on Periscope during their presentations I saw the amazing Michael Cinquino who insisted that if you scoped three times a day you would become an outstanding broadcaster and it would change your life along with the lives of those who you serve on your broadcast. I just about leaped out of my seat when I shouted out "OMG this is what I have been looking for all of my life!" Yes indeed my Aha moment to Scope consistently was born when I realized that I could add great value to my life and to the lives of others if I would just scope in fear consistently no matter what.

3. What are your scopes about?

My scopes are about how to move pass your fears and rock your live streaming broadcasting on any platform especially on Periscope. I provide you with broadcasting tips and tricks on how to maintain a consistent audience with great content and dynamic presentation skills even when you are afraid to show up being authentically you! I also teach you how to transfer your live stream viewers into paying clients. I provide time honored amazing guidance for Life Coaches in how to best severe their clients through creative coaching techniques. My featured scopes are about believing that "YOU ARE A MIRACLE" so therefore I support you in embracing your life lessons and turning your life experiences into profit!!

4. What can new FOLLOWERS expect from your scopes?

New followers that dare to enter Mama Louise's house on Periscope will discover high level love energy along with wise guidance and affection that exudes the "I CAN DO IT, YES I CAN" mindset experience. Mama Louise will provide you with action step skills to move your life dreams to the next level with implementation tools and tips regarding how to WIN in all of the areas in your life with the focus on how to move pass you fear to "rock out" your live streaming broadcasting, along with mastering your coaching techniques for a profit as well as turning your life lessons into multiple streams of income.

5. What do you want your viewers to know about you?

I want my viewers to know that once upon a time I almost gave up on life and humanity after the death of my amazing 25 year old son , yet I crawled out of my darkness into my soul light by inspiring others one person at a time because inspiration is my life. I used my fear, my heart break and my strength to give meaning to my life again and I am so, so glad to be emotionally wealthy, spirit guided and alive again!!!! So If I can return to the art of living and expand my life so can you!!!

6. Why should they click the FOLLOW button?

Wow! Why should you click the Periscope follow button to "Ask Mama Louise" because you are ready to expand the gifts that live alive within YOU! Mama Louise's scopes will always provide you with exceptional content designed to teach you the viewer how to take your life experience along with your professional development to the next level by inspiring others, expanding your business ventures and celebrating your heartfelt greatness with the world.

Top Ten Scopes To Follow

Ryan's Note:

What Can I say about Mama Louise? I do not know how I came across Mama, but I'm sure glad I did. She calls herself the Intuitive life coach. After 10 seconds of listening to her soothing calming voice anyone with a heartbeat falls in love. The first time she called me Sugar Pudding on a Scope I fell in love. If you need some sound advice only a Mama would give you, this is the scope to follow.

Volume 1: 2016

Michael Cinquino

@michaelcinquino

❤ 1,892,964

📷 Photographer | Brooklyn, NY 🏢
Get the FREE Five Steps to profit
from Periscope here: http://
www.michaelcinquino.tv

1	3,587	348
RECENT	FOLLOWERS	FOLLOWING

 Following

Michael Cinquino

1. How were you introduced to Periscope?

I was first introduced to Periscope by my Make-Up Artist Amanda Wilson. She's the one I have to credit for that. I wasn't *sold* on the idea until I met Chalene Johnson at a seminar and saw her presentation on the opportunity there was behind Periscope.

2. What was your first Aha moment when you KNEW you had to Scope consistently?

I don't know if there was exact moment but I very quickly started to realize that the deep and meaningful connection with an audience, that I had only felt onstage as an actor, was happening on this medium. It was then that I went all in and was on as often as I could be sharing my passions.

3. What are your scopes about?

How to do great things - every day.

4. What can new FOLLOWERS expect from your scopes.

I help inspire creative entrepreneurs to do great things

every day. The framework by which it revolves is: Expression > Connection > Influence > Conversion. I want my viewers to be their best self on-camera and in their every day interactions.

5. What do you want your viewers to know about you?

I'm relentlessly passionate about inspiring other creative entrepreneurs. I'm committed to doing everything I can to help them get what they desire.

6. Why should they click the FOLLOW button?

I will never take a minute of their time for granted and I am 110% committed to offer inspiration and tools for my audience every time I hit "Start Broadcast"

Ryan's Note:

When I started on Periscope I was looking for the best of the best to learn from. I wanted to study how people delivering their messages effectively. I was fortunate to come across Michael Cinquino. As a matter of fact, I came across him the day he released his program "Livestream Profit Machine". I would not be surprised if I was the first one to become an affiliate and also purchase his program. It was a no brainer for me.

He spoke with ease and confidence and he took the initiative to develop his own course in under 2 months on the platform.   I knew I was following a LEADER. His content is always on point and amazing. His course has led me to where I am today on Periscope. It can help you too! I would not have written this book without this course. Click here to get more information: http://ryanroy.me/lspm

Maryjoy #PeriNewbies & PN TV's Fo...der #10xLife

@mjcinense14

💜 393,945

http://PeriNewbies.com 🏅
#100ScopeChallenge | ➡️📱 We help
you become a confident Periscope
http://bit.ly/PNGift #10xLife
#PeriNewbiesTV

2	1,747	883
RECENT	FOLLOWERS	FOLLOWING

✓ Following

Maryjoy Cinense

1. How were you introduced to Periscope?

My up line introduced me in my blogging business.

2. What was your first Aha moment when you KNEW you had to Scope consistently?

Itswas when I started PeriNewbies. I started the group to help othersgain the confidence while Broadcasting. I needed to broadcast to help others to use the app.

3. What are your scopes about?

It varies, but mostly it's about my group PeriNewbies I like the 100 Scope Challenge that I have to do everyday to show or explain what the topics are all about.

PeriNewbies TV that will feature other scopers, #10xLife, I will be sharing about the 10 x Rulebook by Grant Cardone. I will be reviewing other books that I will be reading, which I found that others like to hear about.

Of course, I scope about new things that are happening in my life.

4. What can new FOLLOWERS expect from your scopes.

They can expect new and exciting things that are coming within the group, new developments, Meetup meetings that my group will be having, and "how to's" that help on using this amazing app

5. What do you want your viewers to know about you?

I want them to know that I am here to help them broadcast with confidence, that me and the mentors are here to help and support them.

I want them to know that I know what its like to be scared or nervous about live streaming. That its my goal to reach all the new scopers so that they know that they are not alone

6. Why should they click the FOLLOW button?

For new scopers, what my PeriNewbies group has to offer is amazing and by following me they will learn from me and the mentors and the members. I want the best for them, so I will share what I know they will appreciate.

For those who are scoping already, they can connect with my other followers which could lead to business relationships, business collaborations and many more.

Ryan's Note:

After several weeks on Periscope I noticed all of these
TRIBES. I came across PeriNewbies just as they were
about to hit 1000 members. Not followers but *members*
on a Facebook group.

Maryjoy is the founder of this tribe. Her vision is to help
people new on Periscope get out of their comfort zone
and hit the Broadcast button. Many people struggle
with topics, viewers and just overall confidence when
considering doing their first broadcast.

Perinewbies.com is there to help those individuals
overcome their fears and any challenges they may have.
They are there to help anyone new to Periscope.

Check it how here: http://ryanroy.me/peri

Top Ten Scopes To Follow

Dr. Aikyna Finch
#SummitSpeaker
@DrADFinch

❤ 1,374,146

Educator | Coach | Empowerment
Podcaster | Speaker | Social Media
Trainer | Living in upward mobility
#scopemastermind #perinewbies
http://aikynafinch.com

3	3,897	4,298
RECENT	FOLLOWERS	FOLLOWING

 Following

Dr. Aikyna Finch

1. How were you introduced to Periscope?

I saw the posting about it on Facebook and Twitter.

2. What was your first Aha moment when you KNEW you had to Scope consistently?

I loved the interaction so it was easy for me. My Aha was when the hype wore off and my regulars were not there anymore. It made me realize how connected you can get to the audience.

3. What are your scopes about?

My scopes have always been Education, Motivation and Social Media. I also do Friday Night Jam sessions for my Scope Mastermind Group.

4. What can new FOLLOWERS expect from your scopes?

They should expect Realness, Fire, Value and Passion.

5. What do you want your viewers to know about you?

I want to educate and motivate the world through Social

Media. I do this by being a PeriNewbies Ambassador and Mentor as well as scoping on motivational topics.

6. Why should they click the FOLLOW button?

You have a message to share and people are waiting to hear it so push the button and put that message into the atmosphere!

Ryan's Note:

Dr. Finch is well known in the community of Periscope. I have had the privilege to see her leadership skills at work offline. I speak to many scopers offline and each and every one of them knows of Dr. Finch. She is a great networker that has great content in every scope she delivers. If you are looking for REAL TALK, you must follow Dr. Finch.

Volume 1: 2016

Kristian Cotta
Summit Speaker

@kristiancotta

 524,119

#HELPnotHYPE 💯 Action for Success 🍎 Host of HEALTHY SUCCESS Podcast 🏆 💡 KRISTIANCOTTA.com 💡 #FUNNELDNA 🌀 #TAGTribes #PeriNewbies

2   2,253   466
RECENT   FOLLOWERS   FOLLOWING

✓ Following

Kristian Cotta

1. How were you introduced to Periscope?

I was struggling to grow my YouTube channel and gain traction with my online business.

I would come up with content, spend 3 days filming, editing and adding SEO to reach my target audience and I would get 20-100 views.

I knew if people heard what I had to share that it would resonate so I joined the Social Media Society created by Michael Stelzner of Social Media Examiner. Every week they would bring a social media expert on a webinar for members and discuss a different aspect.

The first one happened to be Brian Fanzo (@iSocialFanz) discussing live stream which at the time was Meerkatvs Periscope. So I downloaded both because I knew this was going to be something big.

2. What was your first Aha moment when you KNEW you had to Scope consistently?

There were two.

The first was as I was trying to decide if would use Meerkat or Periscope because I knew I could dual stream at the same time, I would jump on different broadcasts between the two. After about 2 weeks of engaging in other peoples broadcasts on both platforms I had more followers on Periscope than I had on Twitter or Instagram. That told me if what I was saying as a viewers was appealing...what I could say as a broadcaster would be even more impactful.

The second which was really a trial and error was after 2 months of being all in on live stream and Periscope. I started tracking my weekly growth from the day I started broadcasting and I noticed 2 distinct trends. When I would broadcast daily for a week (versus broadcasting periodically with a couple days missing) the growth was incredibly greater.

I also noticed that the amount of viewers in my broadcast would drop tremendously when I would broadcast after missing a day or two and it would be like 1 step forward and 2 steps back.

This lead me to realizing that your viewers require you to show up for them to show up and when you don't they lose trust and look for consistency else. They need what you have to share you as much as you need them to hear what you have to share.

3. What are your scopes about?

I scope about 3 things.... Products, Process & People.

I am the host of the Healthy Success Podcast and a

Digital Product Creation & Funnel Expert.

I dissect how to tap into your creativity and turn it into profitable products that you can sell with ease and automation through online sales funnels. Additionally a huge part of selling and success is understanding human design...the psychology and emotional discipline of why people do what they do and the cause that creates an effect.

4. What can new FOLLOWERS expect from your scopes?

Energy, Education & Integrity.
I call my scopes the #NoBS broadcast because that exactly what you'll get. I am here to Help Not Hype people up by sharing what I know and being rig lustily honest. It's fun and will get you fired up but I walk the walk and I pour everything I have into those who show up so show up ready to leave with more than you came with.

5. What do you want your viewers to know about you?

I want them to know I am far from perfect and I have screwed up plenty in my lifetime but the lessons that I have learned, the skills I have developed and the inner work I've done on myself have made me more capable, more prepared and more open to both give and receive.

6. Why should they click the FOLLOW button?

Top Ten Scopes To Follow

They shouldn't....unless they're ready to take action to create greater results and healthy success in their life. If that's what they're looking for click FOLLOW. Otherwise hit the X!

Ryan's Note:

I was introduced to Kristian Cotta through PeriNewbies. Kristian's scopes are a "No Hype Just Help." He speaks with a calmness and ease. He is often dropping his knowledge with is daughter in his lap. Perfect combination of businessman and father. The beauty of Periscope is you can see many different aspects of who a person is. Kristian is the real deal. If you are looking for HELP: follow him. He's says it himself, "you shouldn't hit Follow, *unless* you are ready to take action towards success."

Steve Gadsby

@scgadsby

 345,295

We are Nothing without the Team
around us. Built a multi-million
dollar business...Familyman...Daily
meditator. Vancouver 🇨🇦 Founder
of ScopersUnite.org

0	1,589	161
RECENT	FOLLOWERS	FOLLOWING

 ✓ Following

Steve Gadsby

1. How were you introduced to Periscope?

I read an article Chris Sacca wrote about the next big thing in social media. I was skeptical at first but got absorbed very fast in the Periscope world.

2. What was your first Aha moment when you KNEW you had to Scope consistently?

To be honest, as soon as I saw the app in action I HAD TO keep doing it. I was absolutely compelled to keep pushing start broadcast. No matter how few viewers I got in the beginning or how bad it went, I had to keep going. I felt as though this platform was the best way I've ever seen for myself to communicate & connect.

3. What are your scopes about?

Initially, I was very conservative with my scopes - I strictly spoke about business, sales etc. Over time, and what I had always really wanted to talk about was the internal obstacles I needed to overcome while growing my business & developing as a person. Now my scopes are a mixture of business, life experiences, joking around and connecting with as many people as possible :)

More recently, I've discovered "Scoping Naked" - pushing start broadcast with little plan no notes. I find the best way to communicate and connect is by being in the moment, unscripted and seeing where the flow of the conversation takes us.

4. What can new FOLLOWERS expect from your scopes?

I push myself to be as genuine as possible. I like to share things I've struggled with and what I've overcome to get where I am. I also am entertained by making fun of myself :)

5. What do you want your viewers to know about you?

I'm a daily meditator which has completely changed my life. I helped create something called ScopersUnite.org , where we bring together people to share their own stories which in turn helps other viewers who may be struggling with the same thing. I literally love Periscope and think it's helping to fulfill my life purpose.

6. Why should they click the FOLLOW button?

I have a very clear vision for a change I want to make in the world. I want us all to take things we're hiding or are ashamed of and put it out there in the world to as many people as we can through live streaming. When we open up like this we'll find we change as a person and are loved and supported BECAUSE of what we've been hiding. This has been my experience with live streaming and I want others to experience the same thing.

Ryan's Note:

Steve Gadsby is the founder of ScopersUnite.org. This is one of the most amazing groups on Periscope in my humble opinion.

I was introduced to this group by Annette Eckelt-Toussaint @sunshineladyNET.

I was blown away the first time I got on a Scope Train on a Saturday afternoon. I was unfamiliar with the platform and gave this very energetic scope about delivering a message with passion.

I soon found that the Scope Train was designed to CONNECT through our challenging stories. I watched and connected with each scoper I supported. I couldn't wait for the following week to share my story and really connect with people. I have since shared some of my challenges and connect better with my audience, while becoming more aware of whom I am.

Thank you Steve for creating this amazing platform.

ScopersUnite.org – Join to CONNECT through your story.

Top Ten Scopes To Follow

💋 💰 TaShan Parks Twyman 💰 💋

@tptwyman

❤️ 1,505,293

Business Consultant ⭐Marketing
Strategist ⭐ Showing
Professionals & #Entrepreneurs
how to Leverage the Internet to
INCREASE their INCOME 💋
www.tptwyman.com 💋

1	2,655	288
RECENT	FOLLOWERS	FOLLOWING

TaShan Twyman

1. How were you introduced to Periscope?

I was on a live Broadcast with Grant Cardone. He was livestreaming from Meerkat, and then he switched over toPeriscope. He encouraged us to get on both platforms.

I downloaded Meerkat first and then Periscope
I found Periscope to be a better fit.

2. What was your first Aha moment when you KNEW you had to Scope consistently?

Honestly, it wasn't immediately.

I was in the middle of a 100 videos in 72 hour challenge issued by one of my online marketing communities when I realized that people where following, listening and wanted to hear more.

That is when I sat down and pieced together a strategic plan to leverage the Periscope platform as my primary personal branding platform.

3. What are your scopes about?

I am small business consultant & master media &

marketing strategist.

I scope about all aspects concerning business, branding, media (all forms i.e. Social Media, Livestreaming, Radio, etc.), marketing (Internet, Digital, Email, Organic, Blogging etc..) & monetization.
On most mornings I have a theme showed called the "Morning Mojo". It is designed to help professionals and entrepreneurs get their mind right to get their money right.

However, the majority of my scopes are to show my audience how to convert their online conversations into offline compensation. (Acquire more Customers, Increase more Sales]

4. What can new FOLLOWERS expect from your scopes?

What can they expect? The Unexpected.
My scopes are a mixture of Inspiration, Information & Implementation.

When FOLLOWERS come to me they can expect to get 100% UNFILTERED truth about what it really takes to create and maintain a productive & profitable business. They can expect to learn how to leverage the power of the internet (via tools, tech & technique) to establish a solid brand, scale business for growth and exponentially increase their income, both on and offline.

5. What do you want your viewers to know about you?

What I share is SIMPLE. No hype or hoopla on my broadcast.
Honestly, I am not everyone's flavor. And that is okay. But I am an acquired taste like caviar and a fine wine.

Unlike many so-called Business or Branding "Gurus" you'll find on Periscope, I don't do what I call "Cotton Candy and Kool-Aid Coaching". I am not going to tell you something that sounds sweet that will only leave you unfulfilled later. What is share is authentic and of real substance.

Look, I'm not here to convince you that I have the next "BIG THING" or the "Secret" to anything. Because I don't But what I do have is principal based strategies and tactics that if implemented properly, will get you what you want: REAL RESULTS.

6. Why should they click the FOLLOW button?

The question is WHY NOT?

But seriously, here's why you should follow.

If you want to hear and learn more about what it really takes to have long lasting success in both your personal and professional life, then you should follow...

Top Ten Scopes To Follow

If you are tired of following Guru after Guru only to discover later they were blowing a bunch of hot air in your ear while draining your pockets, then you should follow.

If you want someone who will always tell you the Truth and has your best interest at heart, then click the follow button...

I could add more but it is more than I wish to type. So just click the follow button and come listen to see if we flow together.

If not, you can always unfollow at any time.

Ryan's note:

TaShan has a special place in my Periscope journey.

She was at the Meet Up group where I saw the "magic" of Periscope. She was playing on her phone like Eddie Van Halen on a guitar.

When I asked questions, she and Carla Jones @1salonsolutions had all the answers. That is when they invited Matt Crane to Scope via Twitter.

Matt did a broadcast and then invited all of his followers to my first broadcast. Pass the scope. I had no idea what to say, but I did my first broadcast and gained 30+ followers and 3400 hearts in my first 3 minutes on Periscope, my jaw hit the floor.

Volume 1: 2016

TaShan continues to support me and help me grow as she drops all kinds of Periscope and business knowledge on her DAILY scopes.

Cynthia Bazin - SmartChic.me

@TheSmartChic

 911,098

Motivational #SPEAKER | Premier
Mentoring | SUCCESS Magazine
Blogger | Get Laser-Focused!|
www.smartchic.me | Student
Development Speaker
www.CynthiaBazin.com

2	1,604	868
SCOPES	FOLLOWERS	FOLLOWING

✓ Following

Cynthia Bazin

1. How were you introduced to Periscope?

I was introduced to Periscope through reading something online about it! I wasn't really sure what it was all about so decided to just test it out one day, and then I remember telling others in my social media community about it. It was one of the best decisions I made for me personally and for my business.

2. What was your first Aha moment when you KNEW you had to Scope consistently?

My first Aha moment on Periscope; when I knew that I was going to scope consistently was when I realized how fantastic it was to engage with my social media community. I absolutely love interacting with people and getting their immediate thoughts on topics and Periscope allows you to do that. To me, Periscope is the best social media platform out there.

3. What are your scopes about?

My scopes are a combination of kick-butt motivation and providing focused strategies for people to step into their personal and professional greatness. I love to provide great value in each and every scope I do.

4. What can new FOLLOWERS expect from your scopes.

New people that join my Periscope family can expect REAL conversation, positivity and strategies that they can immediately apply to their life. I believe in providing great value in my scopes.

5. What do you want your viewers to know about you?

What I like my viewers to know about me is that I am passionate about them achieving their greatest happiness and success and they deserve it.

I am dedicated as a Motivational Speaker and Mentor to give them all the tools and resources they need to achieve their goals and dreams. They can learn more about my background and services at http://smartchic.me

6. Why should they click the FOLLOW button?

I would love for people to join my Periscope family so they will feel positively inspired each day and receive information of great value for their personal and professional life. I love to engage with my Periscope family; it's important have awesome conversations with the people that support me.

Ryan's Note:

Cynthia popped into one of my Broadcasts and I immediately saw the name. I remember saying to her "I like SmartChics".

She not only is smart, but amazingly supportive of anyone she comes in contact with. She is also an incredible Speaker and Coach. You would really be missing out if you were to not follow her. People dream about having the kind of support she delivers. Go see all the great things she has going on at:

http://smartchic.me